COMPOSER
SHOWCASE
HAL LEONARD
STUDENT PIANO LIBRARY

For the Birds

NINE ORIGINAL PIANO SOLOS

BY LYNDA LYBECK-ROBINSON

CONTENTS

ISBN 978-1-4950-9715-7

HAL•LEONARD®

7777 W. BLUEMOUND RD. P.O. BOX 13819 MILWAUKEE, WI 53213

In Australia Contact:
Hal Leonard Australia Pty. Ltd.
4 Lentara Court
Cheltenham, Victoria, 3192 Australia
Email: ausadmin@halleonard.com.au

Visit Hal Leonard Online at
www.halleonard.com

Performance Notes

I've found a special appreciation for birds around the world, and began photographing them several years ago as a hobby. Therein I found a new passion that arose from observing and learning about them, and it began to color my own piano compositions. The pieces here are not direct transcriptions of birdsong, but are simply melodies inspired by the surroundings that put the birds into a special light, or resemblances of their songs or behavior. The pieces are "easy but sound hard," classically influenced yet contemporary sounding, pattern oriented yet distinctively melodious. Almost every piece moves freely from the lowest notes on the keyboard to the high, with plenty of hand crossovers and "easy-sounds-hard" motifs, offering a sense of accomplishment and artistry to the early-intermediate to intermediate level pianist.

–Lynda Lybeck-Robinson

Pieces

Hope Springs (American Robin)
The American Robin symbolizes joy and a sense of awakening, rejuvenation and new life, because seeing them is one of the first visual signs that spring is on the way. The exchanging eighth notes in the motif feel uplifting, colored with simple but rich chord changes and brief left-hand crossovers giving it a little sparkle. The B section of this piece signals a melodic imitation of one of its many songs, a little "cheeri-o" tune signaling a welcome sign of spring.

Wings on Wind (Raven)
One of the most acrobatic birds in the sky is the Common Raven, from cities to wilderness, fishing villages to farmland. Caught on a wind shelf, they dart and spin and tease. This short toccata in A minor enjoys a simple combination of patterns that darts from one end of the keyboard to the other. The three-octave chromatic scale in the middle spins the piece round to the original theme, which in turn twirls its way to the top of the keys. Sounds much more difficult than it really is, very easy to memorize, a delightful performance piece for all ages.

Celestial Procession (Canada Goose)
Over the corn fields, ripening pumpkins and turning leaves, the crinkled V shape of Canada Geese sails across the sky. It's a remarkable and distinctive sight, marking the end of summer and the coming of winter. This Toccata-like piece is in D minor, to be played with energy, yet be flexible with the tempo, as the birds themselves fly upon the shelf of a varying wind on their journey south.

Little Fisher (American Dipper)
Small, plain and gray, the American Dipper is far from ordinary. It's the only North American songbird that is also an aquatic bird. It can be found along streams bobbing its head for food or diving into icy rapids, even walking along the rocky bottoms in search of small fish. Little Fisher's motif gently bobs up and down, and the moving parallel 5ths and 6ths give a sense of a gently babbling brook making its way to the end.

An Unexpected Yearning (Black Swan)
For centuries, Western thinkers believed that the Black Swan was simply a legend until the 17th century when it was discovered that the beautiful anomaly was native to the southern Australian and New Zealand regions. Thus, in the English vernacular, the saying "a Black Swan" referred to anything that happened that was unlikely, or an unexpected surprise. Jazz chords are balanced on frequent open 6ths and 7ths in both hands, supporting a soulful melody in D minor; haunting; tender and memorable is this lovely, short piece.

Phoenix Victorious (A Mythical Bird)
Solo for the Left Hand

The Phoenix is a legendary bird, grand in size and brightly colored. It appears not only in Egyptian mythology but in many other cultures as well, with similar optimism. In general, the myth tells of a bird "rising from the ashes." To many in present day, the Phoenix represents the victory that is possible after a fall, eternal hope, and power through adversity. This piano solo for left hand radiates with confidence and energy. *Phoenix Victorious* is deceptively easy to learn with its repeating patterns in A minor, and mighty, leaping chords. It results in a very difficult sounding piece, pleasing both to the audience, and to the performer.

Sakura Dreams (Oriental Turtle Dove)
At the base of Mount Fuji, a rufous colored Oriental Turtle Dove pecks amid cherry blossoms at the feet of hikers headed for a once-in-a-lifetime sunrise experience at the summit. Like other doves around the world, the Oriental Turtle Dove represents faithfulness, since they mate for life. Their "coo-coo" is imitated throughout the motive's gentle repeating parallel 4ths. The steady repetitive left-hand ostinato is reminiscent of the steady footsteps of a journey well traveled. The cascading descending 3rds and upward inverted C chord resemble the journey upward, giving this easy-to-learn piece a simple, yet gently exotic sparkle.

Sea Dancer (Albatross)
One of the most wonderful birding sights is to spy an albatross, with wingspans of some species reaching over 10' across, gliding on the wind over the sea. They can fly for hours without flapping their wings, and some albatross are known to circumvent the earth in less than two months. *Sea Dancer* is a dance in 3/4, inspired by the delight of sailors who are greeted by these magnificent birds. The G Mixolydian mode lends itself nicely to this upbeat piece reminiscent of Irish folk music. The right-hand pattern remains simply lyrical, allowing for the slightly more challenging leaps in the bass clef. A percussive exchange of eighth notes between the hands is a fun motif—easy to learn yet exciting to play.

Wonderment (Bald Eagle)
The Bald Eagle can fly as high as 15,000 feet, soaring as fast as 65mph, and diving for prey at a speed of over 200mph. They can soar on updrafts of air, staying airborne for hours, and their interactions in the air are both intricate and thrilling. The C Lydian scale in both the right hand and in the left hand elicits a sense of wonder, coming to rest on open chords, as a magnificent bald eagle rests and soars on a wind shelf suspended high in the sky.

Celestial Procession
Canada Goose

By Lynda Lybeck-Robinson

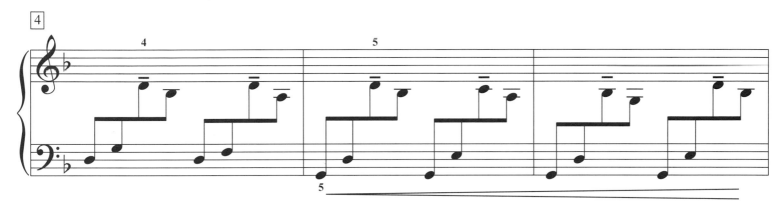

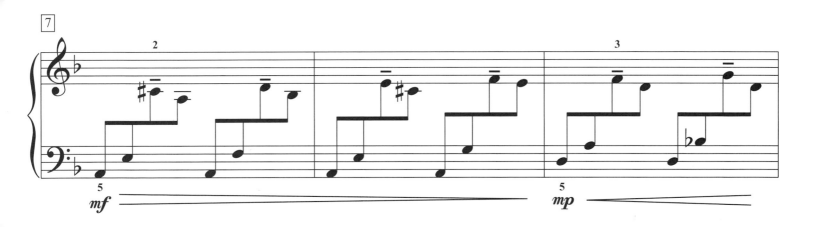

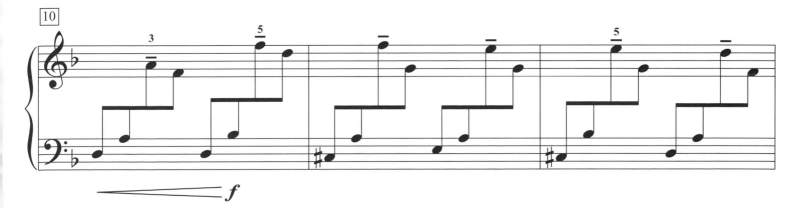

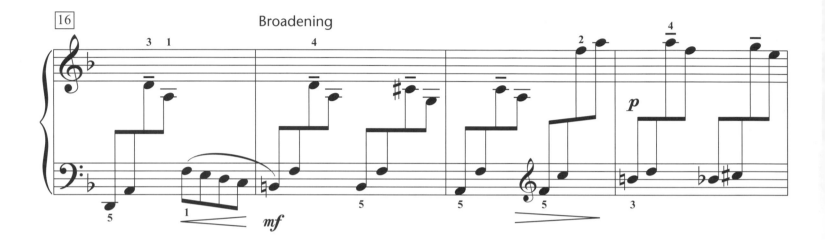

An Unexpected Yearning

Black Swan

By Lynda Lybeck-Robinson

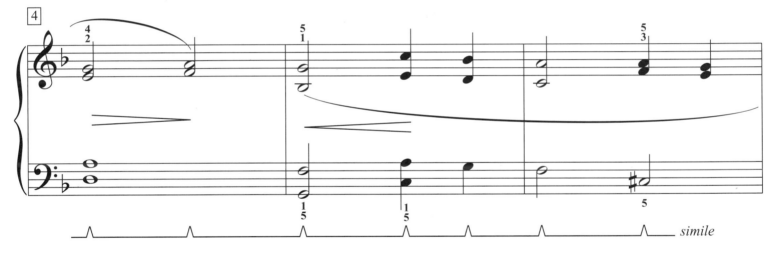

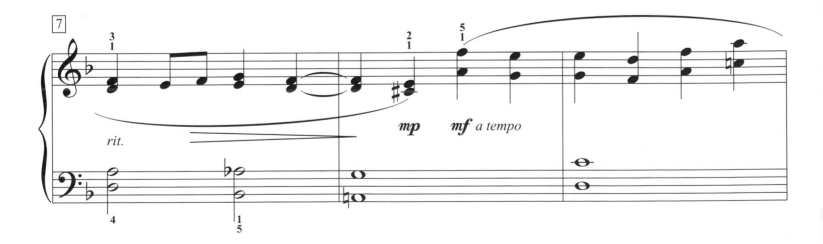

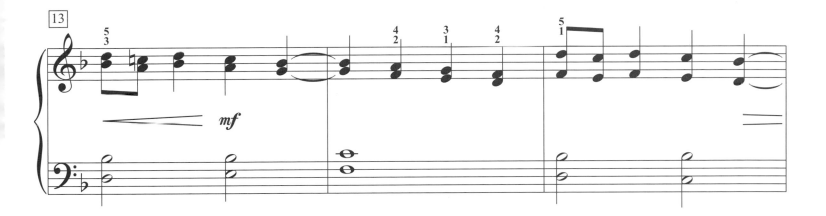

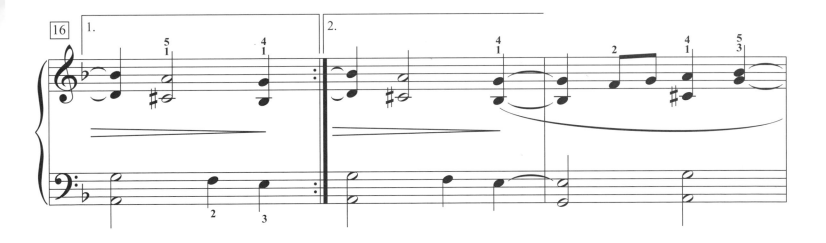

Hope Springs

American Robin

By Lynda Lybeck-Robinson

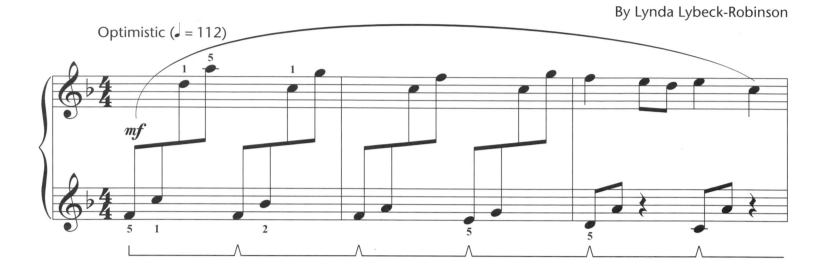

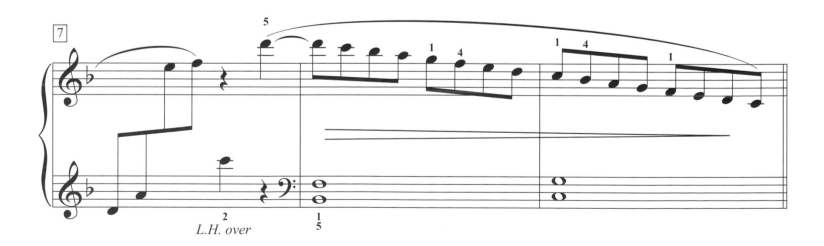

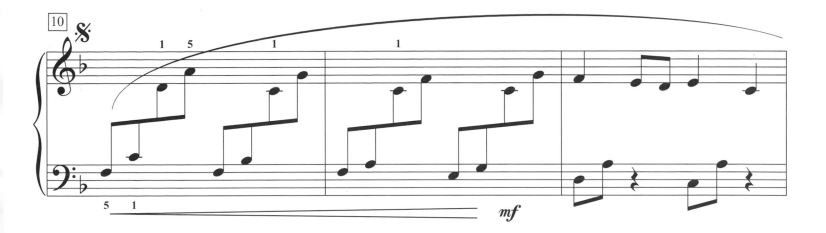

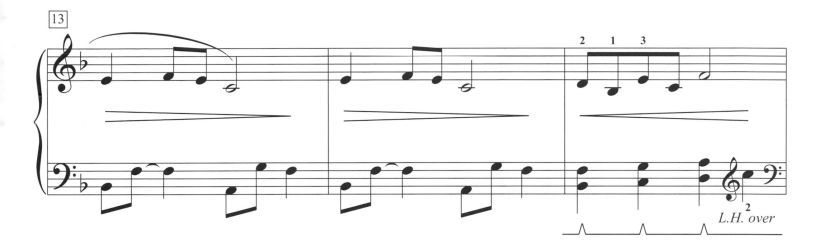

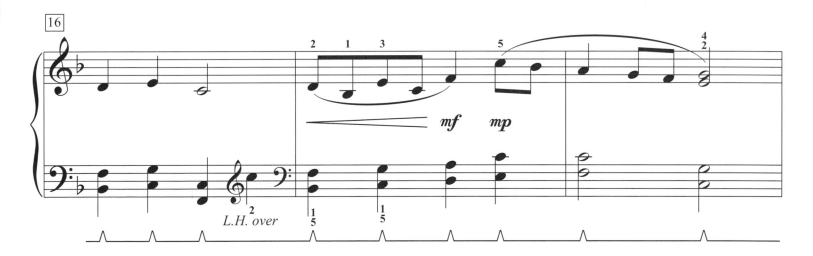

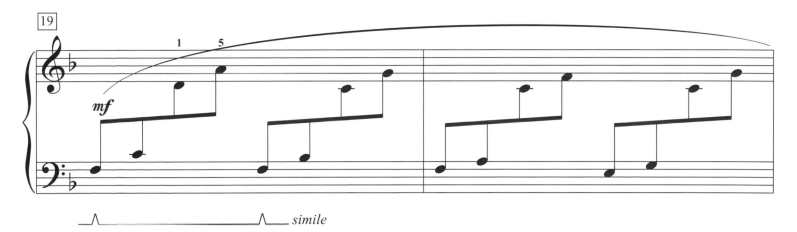

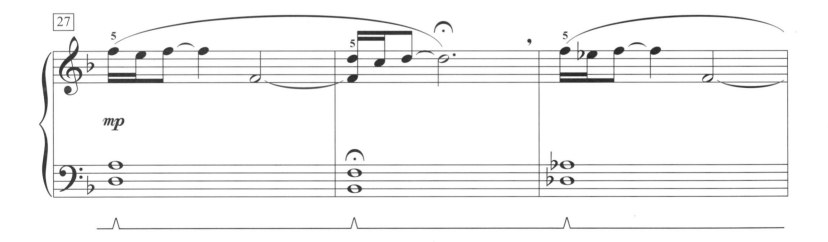

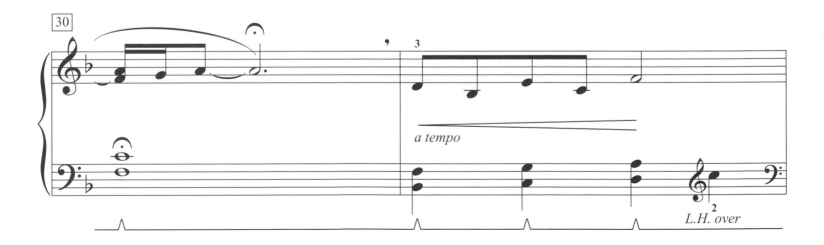

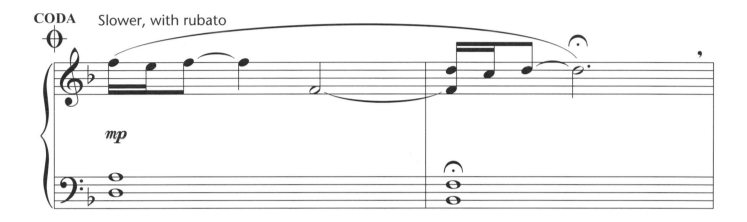

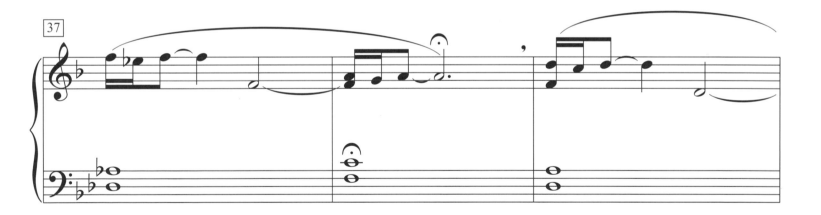

Little Fisher
American Dipper

By Lynda Lybeck-Robinson

Gently (♩ = 69)

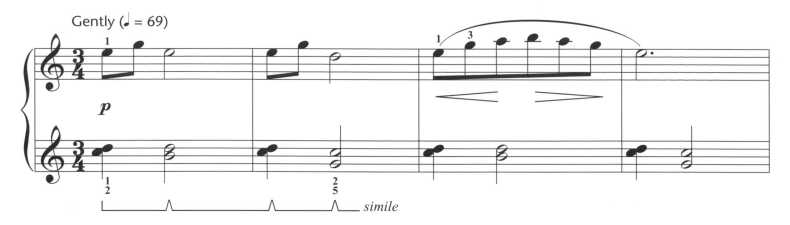

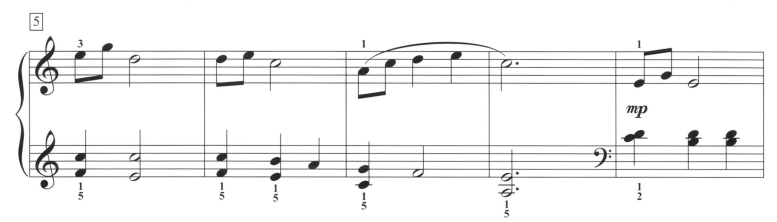

simile

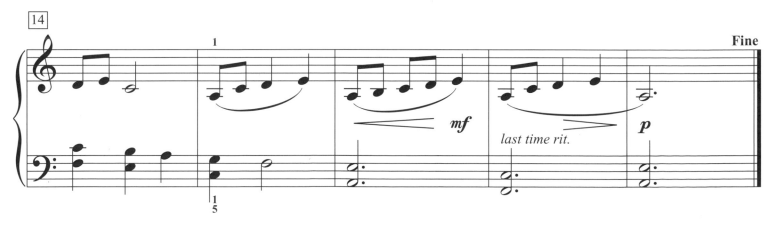

last time rit.

Fine

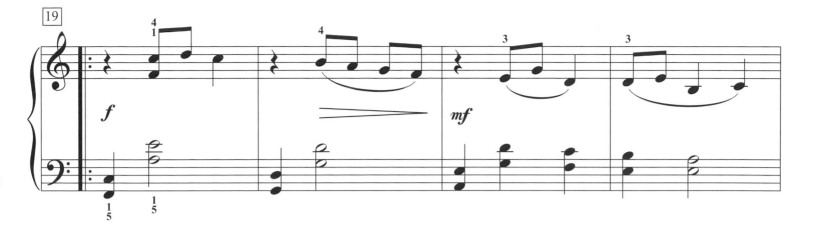

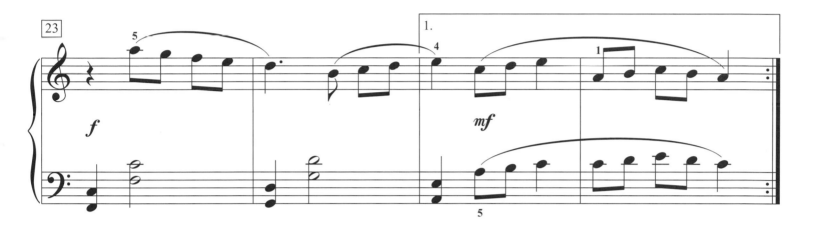

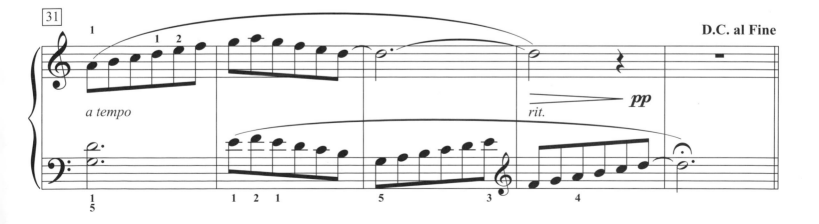

D.C. al Fine

Phoenix Victorious

(A Mythical Bird)

Solo for the Left Hand

By Lynda Lybeck-Robinson

Blazing! (♩ = 160)

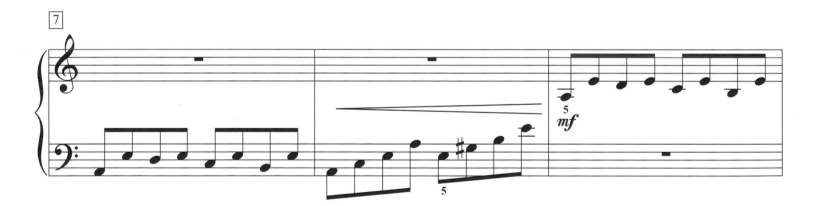

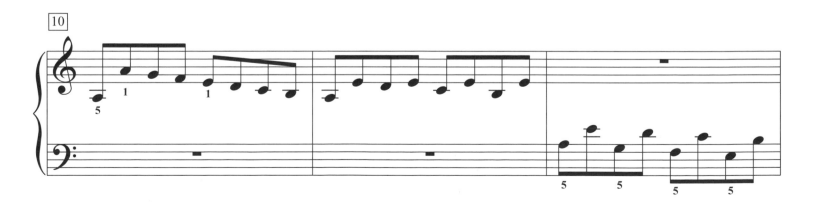

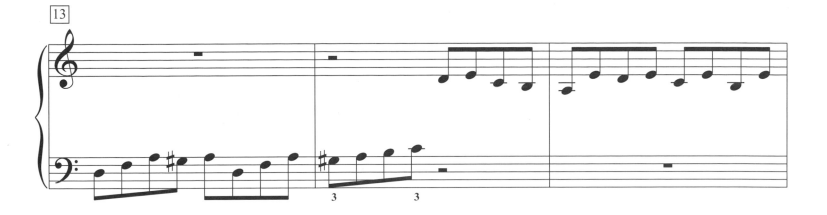

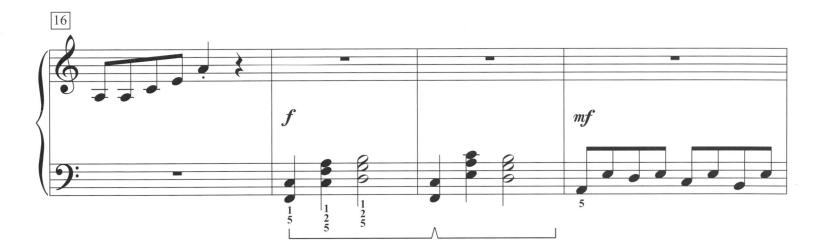

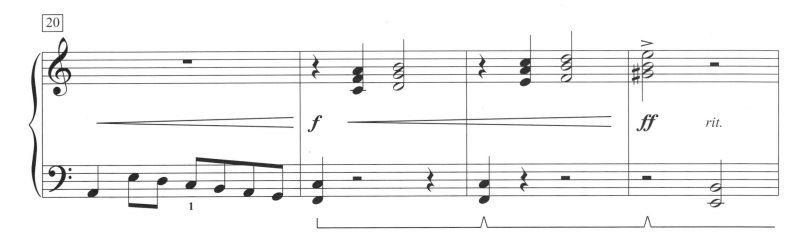

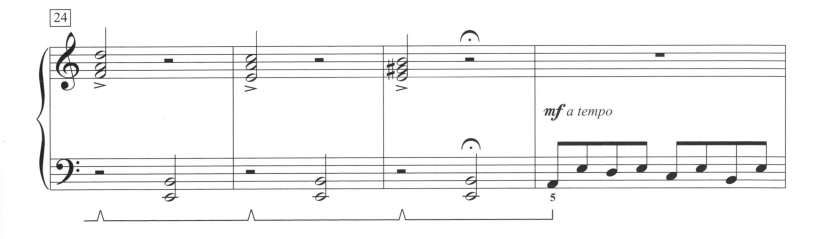

15

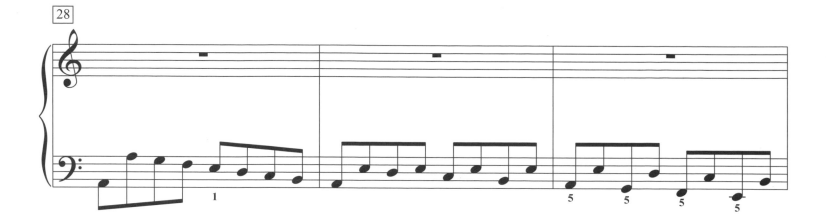

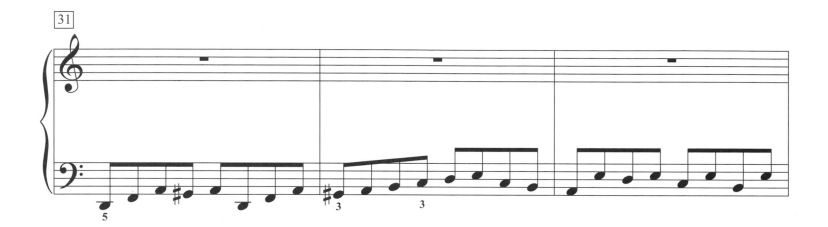

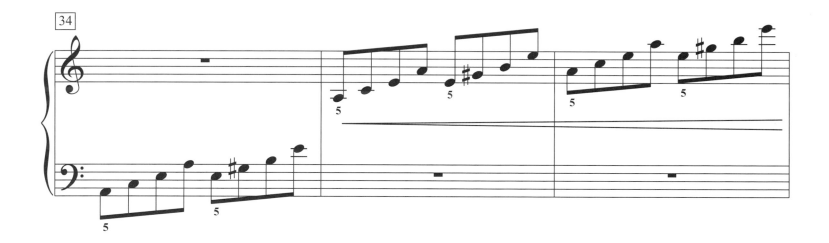

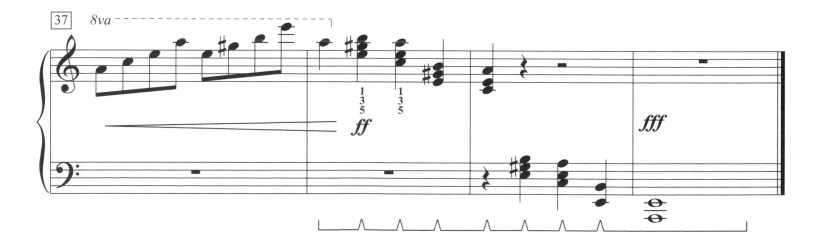

16

Sakura Dreams

Oriental Turtle Dove

By Lynda Lybeck-Robinson

Lightly (♩ = 160)

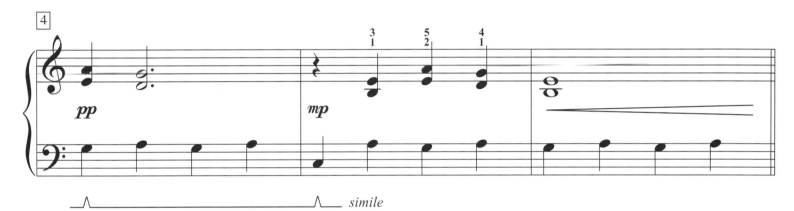

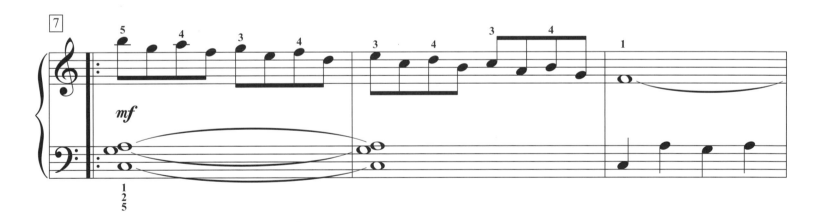

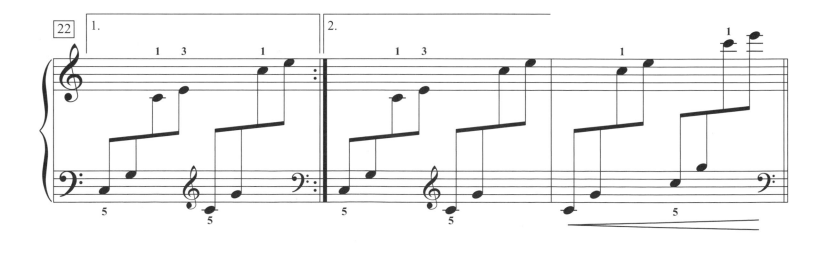

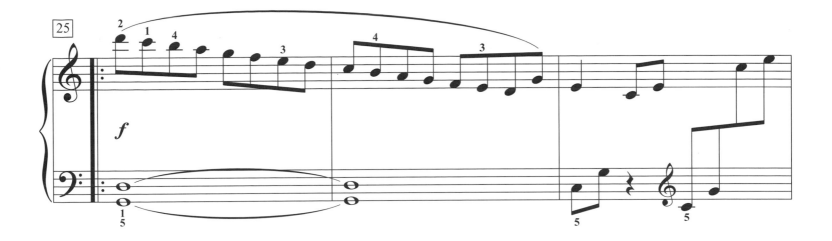

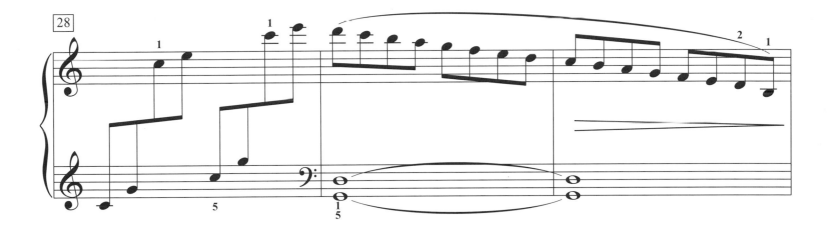

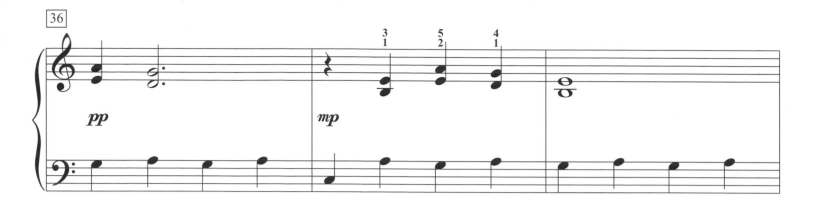

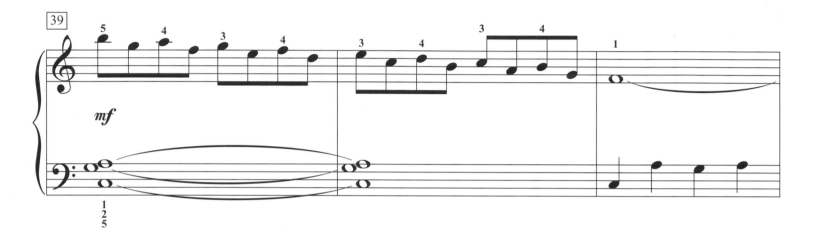

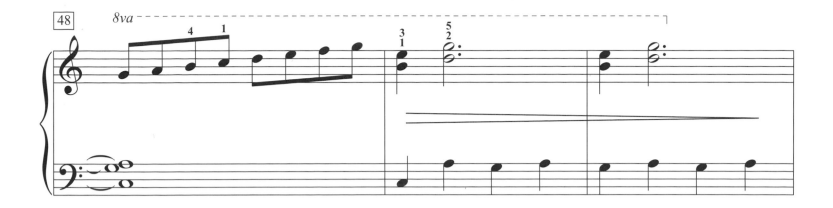

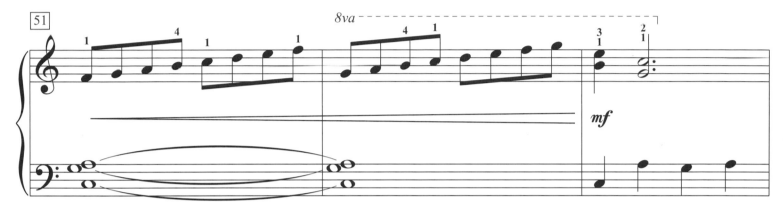

Sea Dancer

Albatross

By Lynda Lybeck-Robinson

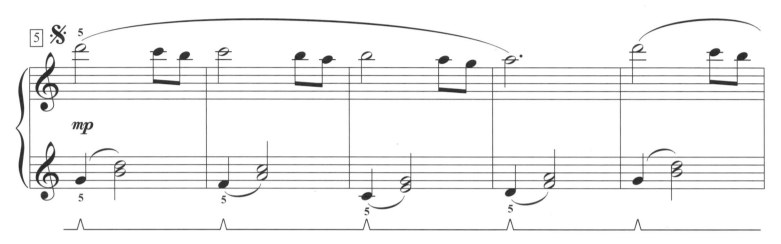

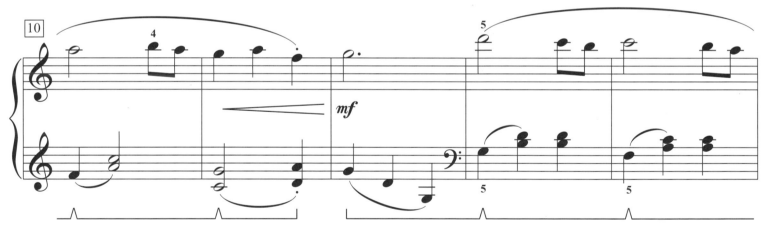

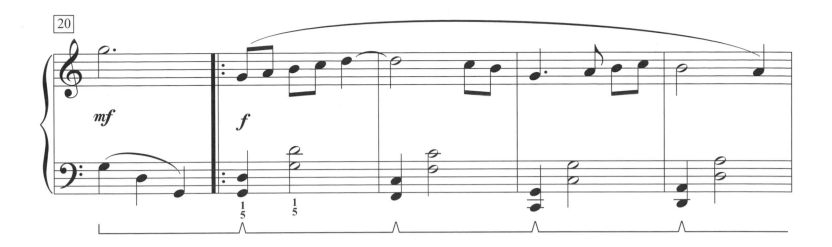

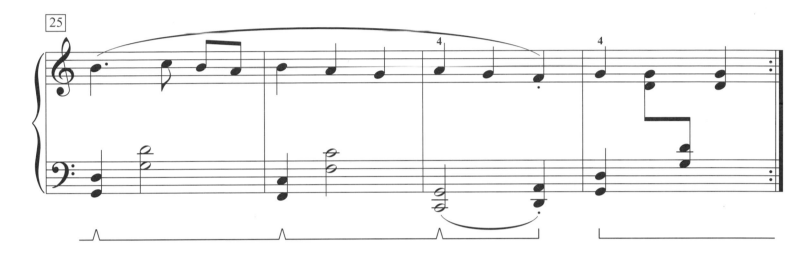

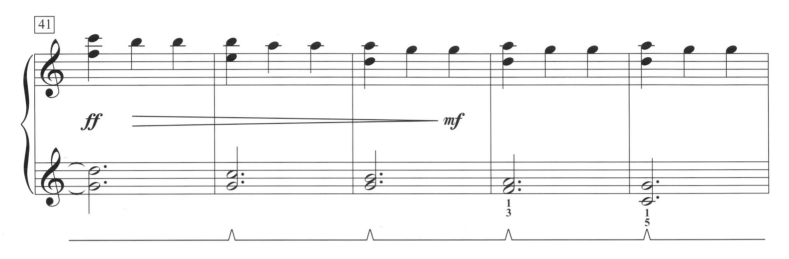

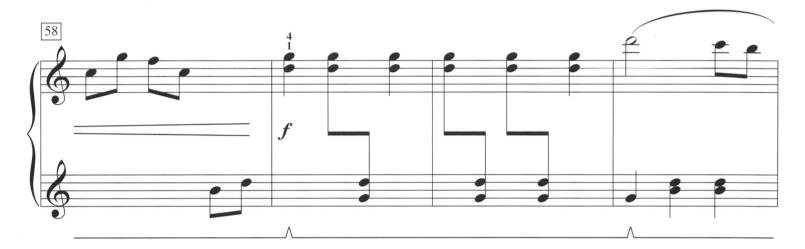

Wonderment

Bald Eagle

By Lynda Lybeck-Robinson

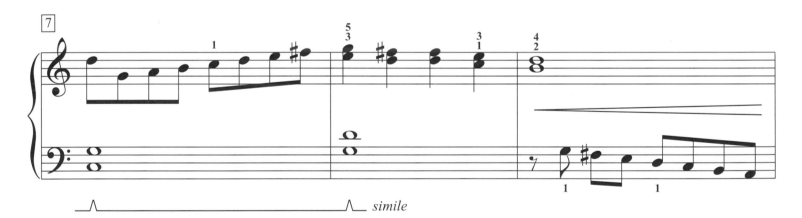

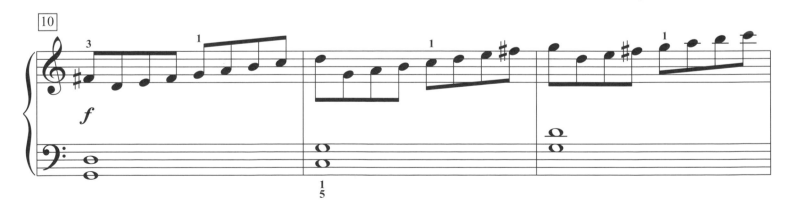

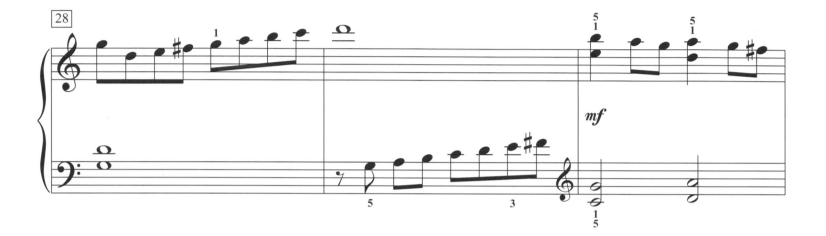

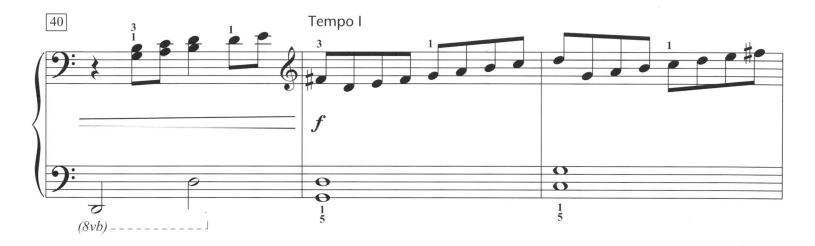

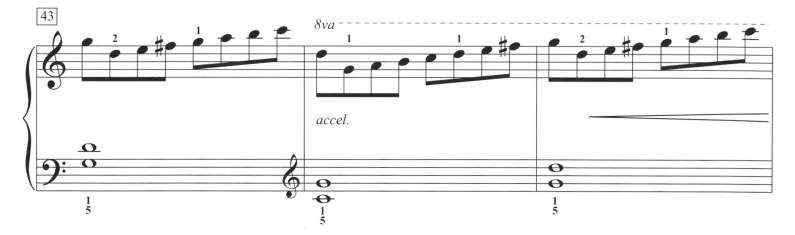

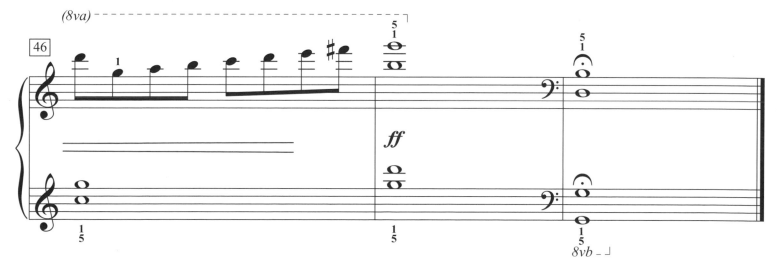

Wings on Wind

Raven

By Lynda Lybeck-Robinson

Fast and free (♩ = 152-176)

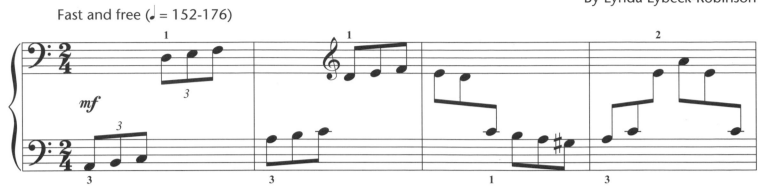

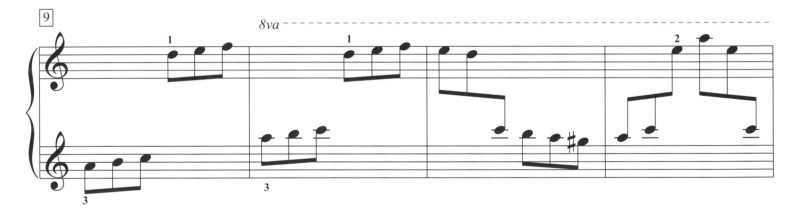

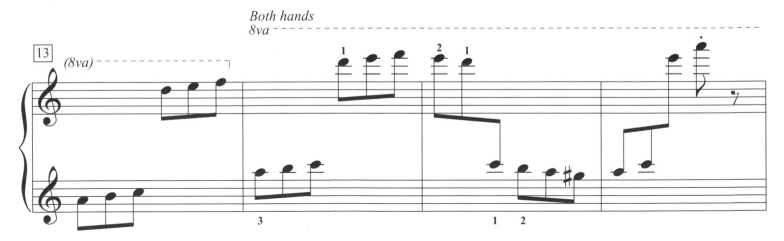

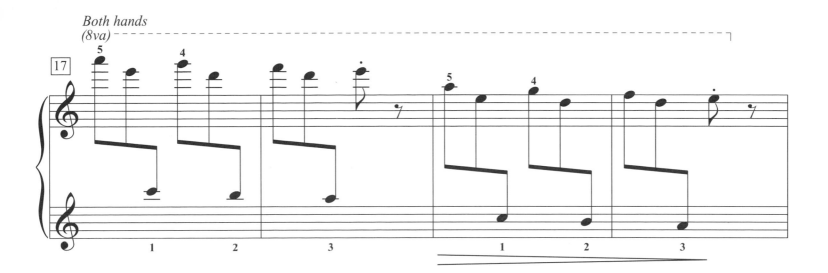

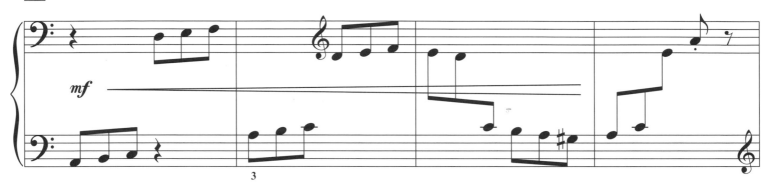

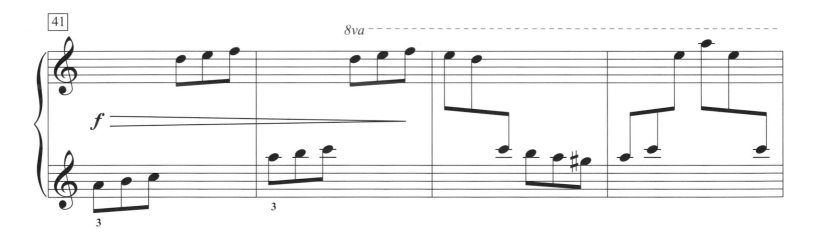

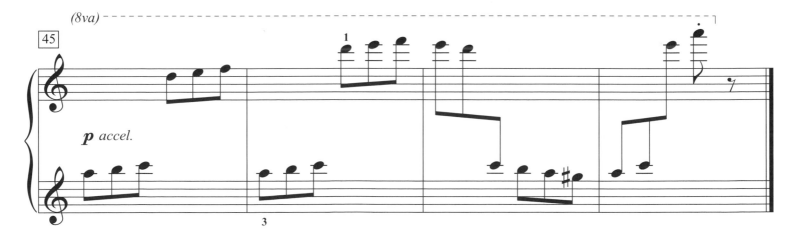